W0016756

Rule of Cadence

Robert Greig

 UNIVERSITY OF KWAZULU-NATAL PRESS

Published in 2005 by University of KwaZulu-Natal Press
Private Bag X01
Scottsville 3209
South Africa
Email: books@ukzn.ac.za
Website: www.ukznpress.co.za

© Robert Greig 2005

All rights reserved. No part of this publication may be reproduced or
transmitted in any form or by any means, electronic or mechanical, including
photocopying, recording or any information storage and retrieval system,
without prior permission in writing from University of KwaZulu-Natal Press.

ISBN: 1-86914-075-3

Editor: Kobus Moolman
Layout: RockBottom Design
Cover design: Sebastien Quevauvilliers, Flying Ant Designs
Cover image: Arthur Tress
Back cover photograph: T.S. Lemon

Printed and bound by Interpak Books, Pietermaritzburg

for Heidi

Acknowledgements

'The Abortion' was published in *Talking Bull* (Bateleur Press, 1975). 'Lady Anne in Time of Border Wars'; 'Lady Anne Prepares to Leave the Cape of Good Hope'; 'In the Provinces'; 'Discovering the Desert'; and 'Out of the Provinces' appeared in *In the Provinces* (Justified Press, 1991).

Acknowledgements are also due to the editors of *Izwi*, *New Coin*, *New Contrast* and the *Otjiwango Zeitung*.

Thanks to Chris Mann and Kobus Moolman for their critical contributions.

Contents

After the Barbarians

The Norwegian Plot

If you believe in gods and ghosts
if you hope for a calm afterlife
expecting to die
soothed by the sea
at castle walls
asleep in an orchard
breathing apple-blossom –
if you believe in remaking the world
and happy endings
you're for us.

All it took
was an actor in old-time armour
mooing by moonlight;
a wicked stepfather;
an intellectual
seduced by action.
And a prince who believed in happy endings:
theatre.

The Supporters of Claudius

No-one ever actually voted for Claudius.
In the bad times
we were all dissidents
protecting the flame of freedom
from others. We were such secret rebels
no-one knew, not even Claudius.

Even the secret police –
they were really working from within
to destroy the system. To maintain their cover
they drowned the odd prisoner or
taught some to fly from battlements,
but these were criminals
and rapists, not to be missed.

Others, the little men, took orders,
part of the larger picture.
They cheered parades,
agreed with the politicians:
these must have been
the bad old days.

Ophelia

Love was all that mattered:
lemony days, willow light,
the quaint cemetery toured
by moonlight and talk –
so much talk – of relationships.
Love, prayer and obedience would do,
and, later, children.

Though it might take years,
an exemplary private life
would redeem the body politic.

The way, perhaps, a pill
quiets the turbulent mind
or more to the point, the rope
judiciously used
will still a midnight street.

Osric

Now he bears swords,
a serviceable man
found near the powerful,
smelling blood.

Once life was pretty boys studying drama,
posters of Nureyev in the bathroom,
first nights at the Coward revival
(a moué for Fugard).

When everything was black and white
one could always invent,
ornament.

Now it's time to be relevant –
applauding the style
of an AK-47.

After the Barbarians

'And now, what will become of us without barbarians?
They were a kind of solution.'

('Waiting for the Barbarians' by C.P. Cavafy, translated by Rae Dalven)

It seems now
the Norwegians are not barbarians.
They laugh a lot,
they're fond of dancing,
vibrant colours:
an earthy people the Norwegians
with a sense of community,
of family.

For so long
they waited for what was theirs.
Now they are here
they inspect our streets,
admire our shops, our houses –
such things dazzle the Norwegians –
they pick up delicate ornaments
with spatulate fingers, even
master our vowels.

And we – the wise at least –
believe we should follow their steps,
praise their rhythm, their harmonies.

We resolve to take fruit
to the old in their homes
twice a month, weather permitting,
to not shout at our children,
to learn how to drum.

Our new rulers have taught us
to celebrate Life.

It is true
we were far more discreet.
We ignored the screams from down the road.
The Norwegians will learn, too, from us.

If we dress like them,
shout their slogans, adopt their dancing,
there will soon be no Norwegians
and none of us, just one nation
world without end.

The Testament of Polonius

I ordered the castle walls
shrouded.
The air was cruel.
Cells sweated silver and green.
You could smell
salt waves trying to enter.

No edifice can last:
corrosion without, erosion within:
we try to preserve what we can,
to comfort, to muffle echoes.

My job was to mirror: smile
when they smiled, to cleave a brow
if they frowned, making no fuss,
to transmit intelligence, scrupulous
in the passive tense.
I secured what was theirs.
Power, I learned, is doing nothing,
is lost when used.

Oh, they will use it.

The Merchants Petition Fortinbras

He will not see them, having other things to do.
Instead he sends Horatio:
his task is to hear petitions
from those who now
have so much to say.

Horatio learns of their loyalty
in a sermon on the virtue of trade,
and veiled pleas for concessions.

He has heard it before, knows their names,
the faces of those who vied
for favours of Claudius, delivered
gems to Gertrude, paid
for the hunting weekend in the wild, for carousing
at fires, who secured contracts for jails,
supplying maggots for detainees' food.

He thanks them for offers not made
and reports to Fortinbras:
'They're shit-scared of new taxes,
of losing their bushveld villas,
being asked to explain.
We might reassure them,
for the sake of the economy . . .'

But Fortinbras, planning another campaign,
says nothing, having factored in
certain yields of uncertainty.

Notes for a Three-Hour Speech by Fortinbras

I

This land only is our mission;
we have no need for illusions
or play. When axes fell the alien
cherry tree, the formerly cold
will warm. Ghosts have no such need.

II

As for mummers, that rickety crew
with scant respect for national borders,
they will be rooted, trained to deploy
the rousing lines by Shakespeare, the bard
of Norway, in speeches by ruling structures.

III

From theatres to funerals –
the subversive rallies of the bad old days.
Today mourning is merely nostalgia.
We should rather celebrate those who die,
the corpses that pave long roads to freedom.

IV

I commend to orators the Romantics
whose rhythms have power to lull the restive.
They knew that this tangible world
was merely a sign of transcendent perfection –
destiny that bloodstains can't mar.

V

Which brings me to Hamlet,
a liberal who thought wagging fingers
would cause the tyrant to cease his wrongs,
ashamed; that concept was fact;
and words could halt advancing tanks.

VI

Hamlet was snared in reflections of self.
He confused tactics with strategy; and friends showing
concern in corridors, scared to offer help,
he considered enemies. He lanced a courtier
but, stumbling, felled Claudius.

VII

By all means, recall devotion to sparrows,
his admiring love of the military drum:
we may revere the thinker when
practical waste engineers are done.
Now we should bear in our minds his silence.

VIII

Since it transcends troubling thought
music will rule, filling the land.
You should con the caper and leap
at Sunday dances. And I may be seen
benign with a smile and discreet foot-tapping.

IX

We will discover traditional tribal chants
for the people's poets to use when teaching
youth to adroitly unroll condoms
and corporate choirs to hymn the good.
Cadence, not words, will rule and be all.

Hamlet Watches

I

I waited in Wittenberg. Watched.
Late, military boots compacting snow
he bisected the square,
Fortinbras haloed by starving sparrows.
I would provide notions, he the arms.

Ripeness was all: late again
he entered after I fell,
took care to avoid
whatever might dull his gleaming boots.
He scooped up the crown; ordered burials.

II

I gape into space
join stars
observe bustle.

The heroes of the struggle
hoist the dead
mop blood
buff floors of history.

They name after me a town
of little significance; erect a statue:
the intellectual, bespectacled, with head
cast down; frail and introverted;
eyes ensnared by ropes of prose.

III

Now I provide maxims for orators –
sparrows will fall in the wake of history;
traitors always think too much;
and visions of ghosts are seldom progressive –
these quell sceptics, affirm the loyal.

I am the face on a coin
smoothened by commerce.
Dropped in sea,
I sink, blur and vanish in blue.

IV

After ideals
come principles
come decisions, policies,
programmes and projects,
vehement carpetbaggers.

V

On Elsinor's walls hang the portraits
of heroes – led by Fortinbras – who rose
against Claudius and ended those bad old days.

More heroes, bulging in suits, carouse
in a popular pub, named *Ophelia's*.

VI

I observe from battlements.

As I pace nights
neither singing nor lamenting
the angels fly close above.

In the Provinces

The Boer War Prison Camps

They also died because they did not wash,
my mother explained. Since we had two bathrooms
and one for the servants, immortality was assured.
She also explained: they trekked to keep their slaves
and slammed, for years, the door on civilisation.
(All history that we learned at school
said much of God, the hairy Dutchman
who sat on air; and boers forbidden to smile;
and crafty kaffirs who stole the sheep.)

After the TV documentary,
its shots of lengthy tents on barren veld,
cropped children and eyes beyond illusion
(photographed once more in ruffs asleep –
marmoreal dispatches to prisoner dads),
my lover and I argue and do not touch.

I say the camps saved lives and shortened war.
She wants someone to apologise for atrocity.

You can't discuss suffering. Outrage is banal.
Victims are bullies in training.
History lifts the blankets, lies between us.

Lady Anne in Time of Border Wars

On every branch, the roses pucker and pulp.
Maybe God can order a plot of drought.
Mutiny keeps me walled and mute, my man
scurries the colony, scrabbling for purchase.
Spinning's for men: my brain leaks out
a sharp design to keep no-one in –
no ghost malign at my centre.

A large mausoleum, cocoon,
the shape of a goose egg, it lurched in wind.
I laid it safe in my drawer where words begin.
It was something to do. Wanting to spill my heart
about pulped roses, preferment delayed, I loosed
a young legion of spiders. They suffuse my walls,
they clutch, they breed. In England they'd be
curiosities. The roses are safe though –
they redden in dust. Till disturbances cease,
I'll converse about crops, entertain gossips
more and more, the fewer of spiders. Who needs move?

Lady Anne Prepares to Leave the Cape of Good Hope

'Off I sett [sic] with a volley of visits to some of the first people, declaring myself an enemy to all forms which in a small society keep respectable people at a distance from each other . . .'

(Lady Anne Barnard to Henry Dundas (Secretary for War and the Colonies), 10 August 1797, describing herself calling on the wives of Dutch settlers two years after the Dutch surrendered the Cape to a British force.)

I

No 'citizens' here: that humped monster
is kraaled by the grey Atlantic. Never ending,
was this country worth the winning?
Lardy Dutch ladies titter, glister –
each has her lover. What else to do?
No masts to pierce the horizon.
Policy rules: twelve disaffected Boors, jailed
a year. A slender case but not
inconvenient. Released they might
play Boney with the border Caffres.

II

I will journey, remove over mountains,
find the heartland. At the caves
no tygers, but the horses reared.
Offered to pluck me a silver stalactite. I refused:
there's virtue in not transplanting.

III

Wine-heated by us, our loyal Boors
shed molar grins and saved the King.
My hands remained unkissed, blued by hunters' hands.
A buck they served, hindquarters stuck in air,
like a child for whipping.

Tight-lipped, smiling, I gripped my gorge
to its proper place. They must be wooed,
not slaves, the conquered. 'All mere forms
that divide us, the respectable, I abhor,'
I declared, quenching the ache for fog.

IV

The desert is noble, even in bareness.
Whispers of unicorns Caffres have seen.
A butcher's man carved the son, broke the mistress' neck, sliced a slave.
Amuck from frenzy, despair, certain death, they kill all they meet.
The Dutch found ground closer to heaven for gallows.
The gash in his chest screamed blood:
they hauled him out of my frame.

In a while, my blood should melt if there's sun.
And habit hardens the nerves not, I hope, the heart:
the heart must leap its island.

In the Provinces

I no longer study despatches from home,
no longer import my wine, learning instead
what clutches at hillsides of stone
matches the juice of alluvial valleys.
Purchase is gained with talk of the weather;
little's in stock, though much is on order –
the roads, brigands and others permitting –
no need to mention except when some visitor
comes with a fuss.

Most at first seem to accept
you can't hope to find panoramas
in a landscape of crannies.
What may seem unusual, even unfair
is simply custom.
And if one day it were gone,
just suppose your business of jails
and all that closed down,
there would be a centre lost.

So one savours
the price of red meat,
even local jocosities
like the murder play by the amateur group –
they're not all that bad
and at least sincere –
or plans a weekend in mountains
far from their pious bells.

Life is so fast in the capital
and replacements are hard to find.
The daily sun has virtue
though it's said to addle their pates.
My eyes are not as keen as they were
but things, somehow, are brighter here,
and besides, like you, I thought long ago
there's not much in view.

Out of the Provinces

I have left the provinces, recalled to the capital,
waiting in corridors for someone to see
reports on conditions grown pale with decay.
Having kept office hours, I return to my room,
study the papers where children and dogs
smile for a future without smoke and fires.

All that occurred long after
plump tributes were echoes
(uniformed children inattentive in sun).
I could say: a few malcontents
from across the border.
I could explain deferentially:
you'll see my report, excuse me,
mentions or warns – in a way . . .

And after all that, leaving firmly,
though still urbane, having said
all I could, even explained what was meant
between my lines, having left them
adequate room for withdrawal –
what could be the new beginnings?

I have left my province as requested,
come to slump in drab corridors, imagining
my name called through a frosted glass door,
leaping too eagerly; the pinched typists giggle.

At the end of each day
I am jostled on corners,
wondering which way.
I could show foreign visitors
some marvels of our 46-year reign.
I still have out there
the contacts to use for an agency,
dealing in exports or imports.
I could even return, living
quietly, an elder statesman,
not without use to the generous.

I used to dream of gardens
with water tossed silver on leaves
and childhood suburbs with strollers,
laughter and splashes in pools.
I have returned to angry dogs, unstaunched alarms,
gouts of smoke over ridges.

I recall soft undulations of desert,
the phantom lakes in hollows,
and, once, in my rearview mirror,
a man – one of them – bent beneath
pots and pans, a leaky mattress, panels
of pocked corrugated iron, going
or coming home. Despite my dust.

Discovering the Desert

When the daisy grass falls brown
and heat funnels the valley
I must, always too late, plan
my water. There'll be no rain

until winter, and winters get dryer
since the flood – no-one knows why or
if elsewhere earth gets more
than it should. That's what I say.

So if ranges don't intervene, and the wind
does not veer or fade into sunset, we might
spend all night beneath slithering wet
clearing the gutters, with that freight

of old grass, dirt from the council's
unfinished road, rose petals, and needles
from the wild-armed pine I should axe
when I've the heart, and birdshit –

though there's no harm in their lime
and they eat, more or less, what we do –
all found by a nightful of rain,
ringing down into tanks. Water to drink.

From here, sinewy blue and silver,
binding the thorn trees, the river.
When the pump complies, larvae convulse
out the tap: you can lave your roots in this.

That's all. I don't know why, for the flow
is fleet, if dun, and my world is beyond
your bilharzia. Though brak with salt,
still cows eat lucerne and roses stay fecund.

And we still survive in a manner of care:
knocking the tanks, hope they don't boom.
Some padlock their taps, carry a gun.
And once I spent summer hoarding saliva.

That's when I realised desert
underlies all, from the friable stem
dissolving to dust, to the river sowed
to harvest gross boulders.

And my pipes gagged out sand,
the tanks cavernous, my windows veiled,
and no care could moisten
the brittle goldfish, nor cause for wind

to douse the sun in a cloud.
Parched even the sweet secretion
where blacks pray, high up in the cleft,
my inside walls, resuming to lime and dust.

Once, as a child, coming round with fire
eating a way out for more air,
a nurse gave me an ice-cube to suck.
Whatever I tried, I would be sick,

losing all juice. Still one turns off
all taps, even in flood, rehearsing frugality,
moves with an overfull glass; too dark to see
and sun burns eye into marble.

Biography of an Ordinary Man

Visiting Mrs Leech

Winter, and snowy buses in empty streets.
The Christmas crowds took taxis, not he
who nightly limped on chilblained feet
to Mrs Leech's down the road, with colour-telly,

asthma, his mother's manner and talk
of her sodden husband and three fat cats.
'The nights are cold and wet; to walk
is dangerous; what will become of my cats?'

He is kind and seems to understand.
She feeds him tea and cake. On Saturdays,
they're at the pictures. He pats her hand
when the heroine dies, and always pays.

About His Room

What to say, then, about his room?
That it was a yard of books, that the cupboard
lodged many hanging selves; in the bed
he wanted to die, and the mirror
was a crossroads named for a rendezvous
both dreaded. In his desk, the shanties
unknown to tourists, except when razed,
old painful letters and photographs uprooted
from walls – so many that drawers always stuck
when he tried to look back.
There was a phone that was tapped
(he swore) so few rang him and prints of 'Spring in Japan'
taken from the calendar of some firm.

A muted ward of fractured intentions, his room:
neither silent nor noisy.

His Evening Out

'You'll love William. And Marilyn is dying
to meet you.' Palms spread, *con passione*.
Eyes lacked entreaty. She was lying,
he knew – so what? Nights were dreary.

Flipped like an unwanted fish with whiskey
(he'd asked for brandy)
before William's yellow canines, the sour laughter.
Ignored, weary of intelligent nods at William's bellow,

his cigarettes ignored. No, he could not say
he knew . . . what was her name?
Marilyn spilt her drink on his trousers – gay
shrugs shamed his thigh. The grin

of his hostess across the room
he could not but see. The noise
battered his belly, invaded his brain.
Was he screaming? The 'boys'

were comparing cars. 'I once had
an Austin, now buses.' 'We said,
"cars".' His hostess had vanished to bed.
Strip poker he always refused.

O for a clutch of women to hang
from his belt by their hair –
O for Ferraris, height, a machine gun
to riddle them all into air.

And no mirrors to mock fear
and no books, no thoughts,
only sleep without dreams.

Heavy Date

After coffee, communication – so important
in our complex times. He agrees, of course;
hopes she'll do something – not too permanent

nor soon to block the crevice up her dress
distracting his discourse of nod and grin.
(Her misanthrope is vehement, protests too much;

the class toady, the dumb cry-baby, still
drive her.) Personal relations! We don't
feel or love today – we must feel.

(She feels too much herself. Dated monthly
perhaps.) He rises, takes his keys, interrupts:
'Your stupid natter bores me. Goodbye.'

Sent to Coventry, through tears she mourns his parting.
The idea dissolves. Instead he stares at her thighs;
leaving, drowsy, withholds the monthly kiss.

The Affair

When I felt her hands and breath upon me,
she seemed a cat and I a mouse.
That changed soon: I bore with
the wet intrusion of her tongue.

They joked about sex at work,
but I interpreted the swells and folds
of her body through long
wet evenings. I liked the thought

of her touch. But that was all.
It did not matter that it was she, I suppose.
I said I loved her when she asked,
and maybe it was true: I'd never loved before.

Asked me often what I was thinking
towards the end; she dissatisfied,
and I resentful of her efforts,
pondering the shape of female breasts.

Avoided me at work, and I
was only slightly offended
(as though she was guilty of discourtesy)
when they told me she had gone.

The Abortion

Too late now to recriminate.
Appalled, each consulted friends.
One said she knew of a doctor who might;
love-making now didn't seem right.

Somehow they spoke less and less,
knowing three months could be dangerous.
Rather the pain than marriage, she said,
but she still loved him, she confessed.

Told himself it had been worth it,
solicitous as a husband, tense
as a murderer. 'It happens
if you're careless,' was all her parents said.

They understood, took the cheque, gave consent.
That night he spent with a girl
he screwed on and off. She would not get pregnant –
he'd ensured she was on the pill.

When he called with flowers,
she was loving and pale, in bed.
No need for the solemn face,
she laughed. Inside he was dead.

'Yes, a bit of blood – not painful.
Feel – my breasts are all milky.'
Swollen eyes. 'Was it a boy or a girl?'
He did not expect her to cry.

He Contemplates Suicide

Suicide was another's suggestion:
No-one would know once it were done.
In any case, no-one would matter;
He would watch them scandal and natter

Round his grave, after the kind
Hypocrisies were said, would comfort
Bereaved (if any) with the golden wind
Of his wings. To hell with it.

He'd write no note. Why compound
The cliché or verbiage some vulture
Would scavenge? Rather be found
Enigmatic, mocking, to forestall a tear,

But otherwise dead. The thought
Of piranha mouths round a hospital bed –
'You're alive – why oh why did
You do it?' – would ensure he did it

With no Freudian slip of the blade
Or barrel 'twixt hand and head. Spoil
Good sheets and clothes with rusty blood?
A pill wouldn't skew the mysterious smile.

Compose the epitaph, then close the door.

Cry-Babies

South Coast Holidays

When I was small, we often came here.
Forgot the sleek, mythical shark that roamed
the coasts of the Indian Ocean, assorted
arms and toenails aslosh in his belly.

On hot evenings, my skin boiled and bubbled
with blisters. When there was rain, breakers melted
and the lagoon stained the sea chocolate-brown
for miles down the coast. Then the beach

was littered with branches and pods that popped
when stood upon, and bleary bluebottles
and jellyfish, pink as marshmallows.
It was then that we should beware of sharks,

the grown-ups said. But we saw no black
triangles, only the harlequin nannies, with
fat friends, who shouted us home
from mud-pies for meals.

And now I remember
the electric cicadas in the bush, the gaunt
derisive hadedas, and the soft dent
of a hoof in the early sand.

I never knew before the ruby hibiscus,
hot bougainvillea, nor the serrated
rustle of banana leaves that invade
our civilised gardens. The spray that stings
on skin and window seems fiercer now:
like half-asleep snakes, the sunning lagoons.

The Undertaker's Wife

I was married to an undertaker.
It's just a job, like selling drink,
being a doctor, helping people
out, he says. I did not disagree.
When I was fair and fond of dancing,
he chose disposing of the deceased.

He would not sleep but knotted
my arms round his sorrow. I watched
dapples cross the ceiling: all night
he shook so I'd know he was there.
Said if I was unable to cry,
they'd have no need to swab out my eye.

He was a great one for a joke later on,
for a while. Business is dead;
I'll be the last to leave you.
And always the one about the stiff,
the low coffin and snapping the penis.

That sent the boys home fast
though they never stayed long,
and I lost the custom of smiles.

Perhaps the taint of formaldehyde,
or the way I could never simply undress,
lie with the night upon me, motionless
till a dawn unstained by his dark suit
drove me to the narrow room.
Or how he bent, digging the garden.

Yet I stayed, perhaps to witness a face
grooved by professional grief, and a voice
that made widows yield all they had.
Or to stroke when I could the ash
off his suit. Only a packet a day would do.
When he came home all grey . . . why
I could have blown him away.

Monsters

Aged ten I was Elvis
Hips eloquent of tousled beds.
I saw below rapturous faces:
Applause went improbably on and on.
I ranged the camp, scavenging more.

I passed a tent where the leaders sat,
Half-broken voices arranging my days,
Heard one who often came to play:
'The way he yowled, "*Love me Tender*"!'
I feigned illness, went quiet a year.

The same one, when plasters were fresh
Off legs browning normal at the pool,
Pushed me in. I had no muscle for swimming,
Wherever I rose fists waited.
Grown-ups extracted apologies: my defeat.

I distrust leaders still, will not sing.
Swimming, I'll wait till all have gone.
Yet when my baby is hooked by claws
In nightmares, I tell him hugs and kisses
Find in beasts, piebald pandas.

It's not so, and he knows.
If my horror and I should meet
I'd revive those roots of hate,
Make him yowl and push him down,
Grind a boot into his crown.

When I lay my baby down
He claims my thumb as talisman.
I can't follow tugs of sleep:
Hope his light will rout the monsters,
Or steady breath lull them always.

The Japanese Wives

The Japanese wives came to tea.
They praised the mauve of jacaranda,
the curving bougainvillea; they threaded among
calm balloons of rose-blossom held aloft
in rows outside my parents' massive
masonry house with its palpable lawns,
tectonic plates of blue light –
the pool replying to sky.

They were anxious to navigate rooms:
so many! With so many chairs,
the kitchen like ones in American magazines!
Were surprised to find, far from home,
prints of courtesans brushing poems,
a Nissan ticking in the garage.

But most of all they twittered and giggled
at the two Corgis, William and Charles,
named after princes by mother
(who also displayed bright coronation mugs
to baffle the arty).

'Like the Queen,' they remarked,
nodding and smiling, trying to make tongues
embrace 'Charley' and 'Willie', who shrank from strangers.

My mother did not mention Deshima Island
where merchant Dutch were corralled by night,
let out briefly to trade by day.
The Japanese painted the large-nosed devils
with rufous hair, spatulate fingers.
The Dutch painted the Japanese
sly and simian.

My father did not reminisce about Singapore
in '45, how samurai swords were not returned
to the bowing generals and admirals
but broken before them.

Albert, the servant, who was not
named after the Prince Consort,
entered red-sashed, white-suited, with tea.
He crashed the tray, ran laughing out.
'Chinese, Chinese,' he told my mother.

She, remembering Deshima, said:
'They find you quite as quaint.'
Being inscrutable, they did not notice
but fed the Corgis shortbread.

The Japanese wives left behind a picture:
a placid duck in beaten gold,
each feather incised,
with three chicks
rippling a pool of jet.

Long after my parents were dead
each January arrived
Christmas greetings with bright stamps
and requests to be remembered warmly
by Albert, William and Charles.

Cry-Babies

When other children cried,
I marvelled at their sound,
the smeary lips turned down
and hanging spit and tears.

There were so many ways to cry!
Some held their breath, went blue,
some hooed and hooed a song,
and some went on for far too long.

At Saturday parties when children cried,
we gathered in a ring to stare
till something brighter came along
like frogs or cake or Punch and Judy.

Grown-ups were often quick to blame,
so it was usually best to run
and hide if someone cried. Or
just call out: 'We're only playing.'

I must have cried and also taught
unblinking children drawn by sound
that grimaces of pain were odd
as a man without a foot.

I know that those who broke
our circle with a touch or word
or said, 'It doesn't matter',
made me want to kick them hard.

Nothing would ever get better:
the stolen toy or coming last
or being left out were there
for good: comfort made no sense.

To Ian

I would hold you close
but you are intact
behind thin sobs
where no-one refuses
and no rains find Bunny
to make her dank, unhuggable.

To hold you now
as I need to,
breathing you in to make us safe,
saying all will be better,
would make us one,
end the distance of sympathy.

But my beloved, my son,
you are a stranger,
Other as patient to nurse,
tribe to visitor who would not alter
by seeing or being seen.
Blood is between us.

To stay as close
as you allow
is all I may do,
trusting your pain will pass
to knowledge, so you will see
though I have no power
over wolves or snakes or people
who take without saying please
and cannot lower every light-switch,
I am your buoy
here is safe mooring.
And there are storms.

Climbing the Mountain

At the summit, flat in shale,
were footprints of dinosaurs. Someone said.
And crazed eggs rarer than Fabergé.
Strolling past the lizard-brown river and up
would reveal herds, furtive among
spiky aloes: rocks restive.

My son's visions are incandescent:
whose genes ignite them?
My father, remote, thin and brainy,
never took me roaming beyond Ithaca.
I was often in plaster: one Sunday
reading 'Kubla Khan', aghast at my snores.

Mastering the mountain between morning tea
and lunch with the cool, admiring girls
had little to do with magical lands.
Perhaps with being slight in the eyes of my son,
remembering the shame of a bookish dad,
wanting one normal and hearty who ran.

I was hardly in search of a break from pain:
it was simpler – wanting to be together away
from games played among roses in beds
or paddling waves tamed within shark nets
or dogfights with plastic Spitfires, or chess.
Wanting to be other than always patient.

We were cosying life in suburban habits.
My surgery made the boy too paternal.
No longer moaning when sent to bed
slack-limbed, clutching Bunny, dozing.
By day he turned the crutches to guns,
called me 'slow-coach'; appalled, he fled.

Enclosed from sky on the river path,
he conjured echoes, stoning the water.
I had hoped for a soft syllabic
movement of air or vowels of current
dense with fish. He would noose dinosaurs:
I would drive them home rolled in the boot.

We rose through green to titanium sky
entered the herd of bald baked hills.
I planned each step, flinching at mica,
no birds, no plants, no moisture.
Over a col, we discussed turning back
to settle for leguaan life at the river.

Could people in aircraft heading for London
look down and see the alarm of his shirt?
Perhaps the dinosaurs heaved and growled out
by night: what would we do if they came?
I saw no succour: we should tack
along contours, not return nor attack
the vertical battlements of rock.

His mother would worry: we were overdue.
Bush thickened and rattled. Now I led,
said save your breath for the hard descent,
unable to deal at once with the rage
of my feet and his leaking fear,
wondering what if we didn't get clear

of the branches I broke lest they clutch or razor
that blue-veined skin – all I could do –
or warn of loose shale, offer a hand.
A rock-face barred us: he slithered up
like a spider monkey, said it was fun,
and offered frail fingers to tug me after.

At the top, he thought our travail was over.
What markers for climbers there'd been were gone,
the animal path we had followed was dim
and still we had to descend, get away.
That's when he began to cry. 'You made me.
I'll never see Mummy again.'

Mountains in our winter are dry:
we sucked the stones, sat still, held hands.
I told him how he had given me courage,
neither of us could climb down alone;
I borrowed faith: 'All shall be well,
and all manner of things shall be well.'

We had to trust, knowing no way
only pain of loose rocks, assault of thorns.
He had so few years of this earth,
was most familiar with roads of others.
Now we must journey step by step.
If only we were angels who could tread the air

and slide down the sunrays or leap
to cushioning grass then ice in glasses.
But we were not Daedalus and Icarus losing
each other in hot chambers of wish:
it was better to go down on one's bum.
So Ian sat upon cactus and I waited

to see if he'd laugh so I could too
and he did. Soon we saw signs of others –
a road and buildings embedded in flatness.
He refrained from running ahead but became
my companion, a Homeric warrior
narrating horror while seated safely.

Yet that night and after, the monsters with stony
scales and spikes that loomed at his eyes
thronged and pursued him from sleep, flailing
my comfort away, till he found steady breath.
By day he mimicked his sitting on thorns –
to see if I'd laugh or cry. Both

I may do, knowing that we climb alone –
and always will – our separate ranges,
close enough, perhaps, to transfer
some strength, to alert and even sometimes
be heard. And mostly to keep at bay
monsters that sever us – or see us as one.

The Lover

Envoi

Love does not apply. We touch
where we would be touched
or refrain from touching
where we ourselves
might melt most, hoping
like shy children that chance
will finally notice,
ask us in.

The Child Bride

Close to my heart you burrowed
hung like a bat, preferring
lulling lung and rustle of blood
to the sky's bright blue.

We thickened and grew
but the X-rays showed it wasn't
my interests you had at heart:
you were there for the ride.

When they came with the blade
you winced and withdrew.
You needed space but you cried
when I needed you.
You vowed to be true
in sickness and in health.

O, you did and you do,
baby bride, so close to my heart
that when you exhale
my blood turns pale.

The Lover

When she leaned forward
he feared she might touch
saying we must
always be friends.

All he could think of
was hoisted white thighs,
an ochre birthmark –
rough draft of her cleft.

That last conversation:
'We mustn't make love ever.'
'I couldn't sleep. I pretended
my pillow was you.'

When she leaned forward
– keeping a distance
saying things just happen
go with the flow –

she must then have felt
pluck of engorged muscles
gusset damp:
the trickling young semen.

Conspirators

We will, after all, be kind
since that, we've agreed, is most
to be prized, outlasting all passion and lust.

We will scour and burn the linen
ensure no stains remain to betray
leaked confessions of flesh,

nor cracks to mar and mark
our white tiled surface
and no smudgy signs of resistance.

We'll plaster the greenstick fracture,
calm the hobbling thing.
You'd swear any break was clean and sudden

as from a fall by one trusting and small.
Besides, in whatever comes hereafter
will be no call for leap and caper.

This thing will degrade:
speedy incision and drip
to still the wordy aorta.

Mourners we'll soothe and inform
of quiet and solemn burial:
it wanted to go in peace this way.

And if one day we should meet,
eyes may blur or fingers yearn:
nothing between us, anyway.

After Murder

If I am ghost and you still live
do not believe I will seep in,
and visible only to you,
disrupt your spread-thighed rhythm.
Nor will I enter dreams and deposit smiles
upon your waking lips or soothe your itch.

This ghost will be mundane
and return your lessons:
wait hours for calls; wake alone and stand
on corners; accept lovers' means

and ends; cauterize nerves against loss;
extirpate all marks of others' arms.

The Landscape

One day I may wake and discover
you no longer inhabit my heart
or where pain has been quartered.
Then memories of us together will be
factual as one cloud in the sky
to be noted only, signifying itself,
perhaps by poems created.

But now we're packed with landmines,
a landscape pocked with atrocity.
Nothing will grow here straight for years.

Notes for an Elegy

What matters goes, despite the naming.
My words conjure, they kill pink frangipani
pinned in her hair, her form a white eddy
in gusts of crowds. Sieving the wind.
Her smiles, they are caught. Now she smiles,
is smiling now perhaps. The smiles ascend
diffuse as smoke, depart from flesh,
vanish. What remains? If there are eternals
they'll make words and keep her.
The wind! The wind off the sea, the
mountain, gusts snagging on roses
at night, inventing windows that shake,
not the shrike, the cicada nor peahen's shriek –
local, momentary dreams. If winds blow so,
I am awake under a roof, she's here
despite the knocking of absence.
When the wind drops, I sleep,
inventing her sleep, a frangipani tree
that will rise if I wake, or go.

Haiku

Each day we die from each other:
flesh falling from birds
lying in long rains.